THE SAFETY OF EDGES

THE SAFETY OF EDGES

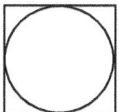

Thomas Hitoshi Pruiksma

MARROWSTONE PRESS / SEATTLE

The Safety of Edges
Copyright © 2019 by Thomas Hitoshi Pruiksma
All rights reserved

ISBN 978-0-578-43835-1

First Edition: February 2019
Marrowstone Press, Seattle

The type is set in Adobe Caslon Pro, a modern derivation of Caslon, originally designed by William Caslon I, ca. 1692–1766.

Cover painting, "Bluebird for Jan," by Galen Garwood © 2008.

For David
sweet beloved and husband

CONTENTS

I

Insight   3
A Word for Speed   4
Sunday School   5
Saying Grace   6
Playing House   7
Old Pro   8
Sincera   9
Speaking to the Bee   12
In the Himalayas   13
Neighbors   14
Self-Portrait   15
Recess   17
Pocks   18
The New House   19
Moving Day for Tommy   22

II

Piano Lesson   25
Hushed   26
Attune   27
Song for Tahoma   28
Authority   29
Invitation   30
Definitions   31
Improvisation   32
Entry   33
Four Windows   34
New Moon   35
Minglement   36
Sabbath   37
The Walk Home   38
Stop   39
Tract on Traction   41

III

Hands Beyond Hands Beyond Hands 45
Pocket Watch 46
Last Thought Before Sleep 47
Peace is Each Step 48
A Just Equinox 49
What the Water Knows 50
Old Teacher 51
Write a Poem Said Hayden 52
Change of Plans 54
Summer Schedule 56
Mr. Berry 57
Daemon 58
The Eye that You See 59
Springtime in the City 64
A Sense for the Mountain 65
Care 66
Cascadian Lyric 67
Prayer 68

I

INSIGHT

As a child I
walked through our house
in the dark eyes closed
keeping out all the light

lamps in the streets
stray beams from other houses
the glow of city clouds at night

nothing to dull
the emptying darkness beyond even
the darkness I could see

I wanted to see
with my hands my body
my memory of space
of time between places

                here
the door
                here
the doorway
                here
the chair
        the dining room table
here
    the hutch whose
edge I could reach
              reaching out and
reaching out

        taking
the sharp corner in my hand

A WORD FOR SPEED

Watch I told her
and raced to the fence
returning without stopping
didn't I run faster
than a fliget I said

my mother didn't answer
not knowing what I meant
so I tried it again
faster than a frilent
a wister a wingle
faster than the words
I invented on the spot

not knowing my invention
meant nothing to my mother
who watched without
seeing what I said

SUNDAY SCHOOL

In my childhood bedroom
stuck to a closet a poster
said boldly in my own
block printing I will be with you
always till the end of the age
followed by the name Bartholomew

I thought Bartholomew
was a book in the Bible
though I haven't found it in any Bible

even then it confused me
because what was this age
and how could anyone be anywhere
always and didn't that contradict
not being there at the end

night after night I saw it
from my bed this odd reminder
of something I didn't get
but it taught me Bartholomew
as the full name of Bart and it gave me
the thought for the first time
I remember that this age
may not be the only one
we have and not everyone
will be there when it's over

SAYING GRACE

At our first house on 39th
the willow that wept
could clog up a pipe
in the sewer beneath us

if it rained the water
backed up through the drain
carrying old shit
to the feet of my father

I could see how he felt
when he showered before work
so one night before dinner
when we each shared a prayer
I prayed for what I wanted
not knowing how to say it

dear God I said praying
my hands held before me
please make the toilet feel better

my mother and my father
chuckled at their son who felt
a little sheepish but also
understood and my family
all laughed at the prayer for the toilet
and did feel better for a time

PLAYING HOUSE

We used to build houses
my sister and I
out of sheets and old
boxes in the down-
stairs basement

sheets I believed were
designed for this
not for the dining-room
floor beneath chairs
let alone for covering our beds

their right use was building
new houses new spaces
rooms within rooms with
roofs sloping in translucent
above our two heads

what power did we seek
what world did we want
what home did we hope
to make below ground

for what family what kids
what friends did we build
playing alone out of sight

OLD PRO

Her table's surrounded
at the end of twelve tables
where the people walking past
between playing and eating
can see how many others
have gathered before her

she works with ease and
unvarnished confidence
dealing the cards without
undo finesse her straight
and gray hair trimmed
short at her shoulders
framing her wrinkled
but unwearied skin

everyone here thinks they will win

she knows it too and she knows
the true odds but has seen
too many losses for
one more to worry her

and she deals and she smiles
and the people smile with her
playing the cards they've got

SINCERA

Rising early
            in Columbus
writing before dawn
                    I would wander
in the dark
            to the kitchen
to drink water
            before mounting
the old stairs
            once more to my room

my room faced the street and
                              anyone
below it
        passing in the dark
could see
        the bright
triangle
        of my window

one morning
            before six
I heard a sharp knock
                    and
foolishly
        strangely
went down to answer

                        she tried
to explain on
            the newly
bright porch
            how she worked
raising money
            by selling CDs

    to help women
                buy makeup
a charity
       she said
and held up
             the small set
of CDs
        to the light
the black
          and clear vinyl
of the torn cover
                peeling

her name
         she told me
was Sincera

            sincerely

and despite
           all the signs
of duplicity
            of warning
despite the dark hour
                  and sharp
knock on the door
              despite
all I knew
       I liked her

she had guts

          gall

she came
          twice more
always
          before dawn
till I found
          the right words
to turn her
          away

we are not
          I said slowly
interested

          and she heard
what I was saying
                    and didn't
come back
          though the mornings
were less bright without her

SPEAKING TO THE BEE
after poem 2 from Kuṟuntokai, *a classical Tamil anthology*

You who live learning
this pollen from that

tell me he says
drunk with his love

have you seen have you known have you smelt
that smell
rising from her hair passing
through the air
beyond me

is there any other
like it in the world

and the bee
of the poem
buzzes beyond reach

like the girl the boy loves
passing through the poem
leaving only
her sweet fragrance behind

IN THE HIMALAYAS

Once in Kasumpti I sat
in the Buddhist temple bowing
when they bowed drinking
the butter tea listening to the prayers
and chants I couldn't chant
when I noticed a young boy
barely filling his monk's robes
waiting for the lamas to
look the other way

                when they did
he took the curved mallet
at his side meant in the temple
for striking the brass gongs
and struck another monk
lightly on the shoulder lifting
his attention from the singing
of the sutras and the incense
and the great long horns

all at once the small temple
became real

           I saw the distance
from its hall to my childhood
wasn't any longer than the mallet
of that monk who was also
myself in the pews of our church
searching my pockets
for paper for pennies for
anything to catch my attention

NEIGHBORS

Next door the child screams
with a sound beyond time
saying what she cannot yet
say in any words
      and her brother
screams back
    seven years her senior
saying without saying it
he hasn't gone away
      he too
has a voice
   though his face
doesn't beckon doesn't peer
at the people with unabashed
wonder
    the neighbors
don't take him by the hand
for a walk
    so all he can do is
scream at his sister
      not knowing
his place is as solid as hers
who will soon lose her voice
and the light in her face so that
later she can find it
to become who she is

as he'll have to do
in his own time his own way
freeing what is his
and has been all along
in the time beyond time
where his sister still lives

SELF-PORTRAIT

As a child I drew pictures
of our house from the front
tracing its lines with twelve
colored pencils on sheet
after sheet of wide paper

our driveway was long
and our home built along it
so I'd sit back as far
as the pavement would allow
trying to see the house whole

in front
        a lone fir
bushes
        above rocks

a gray
        cement walkway
leading
        to our door

a lamp
        on a post
almost
        a pagoda

again and again
                I drew them

I rendered the roof
with gray and black shingles
I shaded the sides
dark brown and dark white
I sketched out the leaves
with gestures of green like

the grass that I glimpsed
above the low bushes
leading to the fence
that led to the back

I never drew anything
from the back

the front was our house
as I saw it as a child
the home I assumed
would always be ours

where even the hours of
drawing and shading
were hours
that could never be lost

RECESS

The great mystery of our yard
wasn't the green grass but the earth
in shadows below the back deck

at the edges grew ferns but beneath
the long planks there were only
long grooves that were formed by rain falling

even in summer we felt the damp dirt
we saw the brown planks
overhead without looking

light couldn't enter except in long lines
tracing the water that dripped in big drops
even when the water wasn't there

POCKS

Look Dad I said
as he climbed up the stairs
I have my own chicken pock
do you see it

        I raised
my red t-shirt to show him
my belly where a single red blister
had risen that day

          no
my dad said that's not
what you think but I knew
what it was without knowing
what I knew

soon I had marks
all over my young body
even on my head where they
tangled with my hair

and I added the S
to the pock that I had
since now I had
more than just one

THE NEW HOUSE

I knew the walls of our house
the bricks of our fireplace
the ledge overlooking the stairs
and front door the way
water beaded at the bottom
of our windows above
the metal strip and rubber seam

no place on earth
could equal it

so when I went door
to door to sell tickets
to the expo the boy scout
expo I'd never been to
myself I could see as
the door opened
to a house up the street
a place that could never
be home

the carpet was yellow
like leaves that were dying
the bricks were unkempt
uneven at the edges
thank God I don't
live here I thought
without thinking and went
on my way the people
buying nothing

how could I know
we'd move here ourselves
when our mother unerringly fell
for the acreage and the size
and the rooms that were empty

my father believed
she could use some more space
and we'd live as before
without piles overflowing

how could he know
what I'd feel in that place
where the walls said nothing
of who we'd once been

the windows looked out
at a fence and a yard
where no one I knew would see me

still for a time
I enjoyed the new things

the blender in the counter
that worked a few months
the shoot for the laundry
that scratched up my sides
the intercom radio that
worked as long as the blender

at first we pretended
everything was fine sitting down
at the table in our new
and clean dining room
spotlights in canisters
dimming overhead

I wanted to believe it
this play we enacted
and at times I did
for we did have more room
and even when my father
hit the table with his fist
rattling the plates on the mats
all around us even then I could think
the moment would pass
without leaving any traces
on the walls

MOVING DAY FOR TOMMY

They emptied the house
on Saturday when I was gone
leaving more room and more walls
than before

        coming home
it wasn't ours
        the landmarks
were missing
        the chairs
the tables the sofa
the piano
        and I walked
from end to end of the rooms
I once knew the novelty
disguising the ache that I'd feel
when we left our home forever

II

PIANO LESSON

The favorite babysitter Carlotta
taught him his first song beyond
chopsticks and the lick
with the black keys and a fist

he liked how it sounded
moving up the long keyboard
his first sight of arpeggios
before anyone had named them

he loved the great magic
he felt when he played
the power and patterns unfolding
from his fingers and he learned

half the piece before his parents
came home he stayed up
to show them the music
he could play

but they didn't seem to hear it
the light that he heard
and soon his own mother
began teaching correctly

showing which fingers
were meant for which notes
and they yelled at each other
till all they could hear was noise

HUSHED

In the library the young girl
her mother checking email
sang a little song she was
making in the moment it wasn't
being sung for her mother
or herself it wasn't being sung
for anyone around her it was only
being sung for the sake
of being sung her heart and mouth
moving in the movement of the song
and I knew who she was
beyond what I knew she was me
as a child singing to be singing
and I knew that her mother
in the library would stop her
would tell her to be quiet
how could she not but oh
for the singing that seeks
no applause and is ours
even in the silence

ATTUNE

The better the instrument
the more clearly we hear
all of the music the player
lets out and all he or she
keeps in

        and why wouldn't we
keep the best part of our song
not knowing if the world
would hear it aright or be able
to take it all in

SONG FOR TAHOMA

The mountain is out
the mountain is in
the mountain is
mounting the stairs

the mountain is staring
askance at the stars
we see by chance
unawares

        in the dark
as we sleep   the mountain
is there   beyond clouds beyond rain
the mountain is there   beyond even
its sight in clear
morning air   the mountain
the mountain is there

the mountain is out
the mountain is in
the mountain is mounting
the crest of the hill

the crest of the hill that is there

AUTHORITY

The first day it's warm
the boy runs outside
                wearing
a tank top and his short
blue shorts
          but it's sixty
they say
        and he tries
to believe them
              but the words
don't match what he feels
on his skin
            his arms both
reaching for the sky

INVITATION

You awake before
daybreak before
daring to arise
before dawn has unfurled
its long and white fingers

a gift you once thought
an offering an opening
though you took it
less and less as old lessons
receded leaving you
yes for a time

now it is here again
awake in the darkness
extending its hand without
effort or strain

saying in the silence
it's yours if you take it
if you take it
it will take you again

DEFINITIONS

May day means meetings
means workers means work
means mornings of bird song
mornings of light means
making new meanings of
meanings in sight means
singing a song we can't see

IMPROVISATION

only happens
                    when it happens

though years may have passed
      so what happens
might happen

the musician who gets it right
        gets it right
                right now

        don't wait
when it happens
        happen

ENTRY

In the prison with its gates
humming open humming closed
circles of barbed wire
brighter than sunlight
everything revolved
around two pairs of words
in here as opposed
to out there

    even
when no one said it
we all said it

    the walls
the white tables the windows
of the mess the passes
pinned to our outermost
garment everything
every thing said it

you are there and we are here
we are here and you are there
for here is where here
becomes there becomes there

there where we aren't
here where we are

here where we aren't
and are

FOUR WINDOWS

1

They say there's no truth

Is this true

2

They say there's no meaning

Do they mean it

3

They say there's no point

Can they make it

4

They say there's no use

Using words

NEW MOON

Some days
nothing comes

and though nothing
is not nothing

I forget and
leave the door closed

MINGLEMENT

Bare
        by the windows
                the wooden chair waits

restful
        restless
                waiting

without waiting
        ready for anyone
                and no one

we sit
        and it stands
                we stand

and it sits
        it holds
                all it can

and no more

SABBATH

As night falls on Sunday
the floor swept the rug clean
I can almost imagine
the whole world at peace
without oceans dying out
whole peoples disappearing
fire and smoke rising
as we race to the finish
where all that we know
will be finished

how can one sleep in peace

and yet we must sleep
to keep rising awake
able to walk and
work another way
where resting at evening
as the sun falls away is
peace is enough
is a world in itself
working to be whole
once more

THE WALK HOME

The willow where
                the road turns
turns white
        pure white
one week
        at the most
each year

        blossoms
brighter than song

how I long
        each season
for their sudden
            soft silence
the quiet and
        glorious
way they appear

            even
when they're gone
they're here

        there
beyond branches
            barren
in winter
        waiting
for a change in the air

STOP

At 3rd and Seneca
waiting for the bus
watching the sign saying
the minutes remaining
I'm standing in the nowhere
between now and arrival
knowing nothing but the passing
of numbers on a screen

how many times have I
waited at this stop
watching the dark buses
moving and then stopping

another in the distance
passes another bus
passing another light
between streets and buses

what else to do but wait

I ask it out loud
what else can I do
and a voice in my head
says stop

there is more here now than you
know

so I stop and I turn
from the sign and the distance
and suddenly above me
lit by a streetlight
I see a city tree
beginning to awaken

      its branches
              a dark etching
      beneath
          a dark sky
      full of angles and corners
      no two alike

      each limb
           below
      unfolding new leaves
      and above
             and above
      tiny white buds
      as fully
           here now
      as they will be
               in bloom
      and as tiny white
                  petals
      when they fall

      returning to the stop
      the streets turn to me
      filling and overflowing
      with new budding trees

      trees I didn't see till I saw
      what I missed

      waiting at the stop without stopping

TRACT ON TRACTION

The gravel pulls free
of the hard-packed drive
pebbles and dust in
clouds behind cars

the harder I pump
the wheels of my bike
the more they slip
on the slope going up

I feel the sun shift
in the shifting beneath me
feel the dry earth
letting go of its grip

the rain we await
is more than just water
it is earth
staying steady below

III

HANDS BEYOND HANDS BEYOND HANDS

This hand has come
from the hands of my parents
coming from the hands of their parents in turn

this much I know
easily enough my grandparents'
hands in my hands

but their hands came too
from hands beyond hands
coming from hands
beyond hands
we can only imagine
though without them
we would have no hands

these link to those
as day links to night
as death links to life
as life links to light

a chain of small links
that link beyond time
all of it here in our hands

POCKET WATCH

Each day when I remember
I wind the old watch
hanging from its stand
where it watches my desk

you told me you liked it
Grandpa remembered
take it you should have it
Lloyd fixed it last year
it runs well enough for its age

and it does
        it stands
at the edge of my mornings
running and still

                if I listen
I can hear
        what he told me
about life
        time passes
faster than you think

remembering his voice
I take the old watch
wind it renew it set it
on its stand

            and dare
to enjoy the time
that I have that I know
won't last forever

LAST THOUGHT BEFORE SLEEP

Would it be so strange
so lavish so rare
to wake to the rain
lightly overhead
both of us warm
in the same bed

PEACE IS EACH STEP

If only Othello
hadn't doubted his wife

if only his wife
hadn't doubted Emilia

if only Emilia
hadn't doubted herself

there would be
no tragedy

no Iago
to torment us

believing he alone
cannot be believed

A JUST EQUINOX

Does virtue equal vice
as day equals night
when the day and the night
are twins

        if so
Iago's right and the whole
can mean nothing
                    except that
virtue never wins

WHAT THE WATER KNOWS

Even in waves
the water fights nothing

it pounds without effort
it slides without slipping

it picks up the sand
and lets the sand go

even in movement
it is still

OLD TEACHER

It's the same mountain
I've known from the water
white and majestic solid and floating
but still as I travel from one here
to another I see her all at once
between trees in a valley

how could my breath not
fly from my body a silent
effervescent song of praise

as solid as the earth as stone
as hardest rock and yet moving
with an ease unknown among men
save men and save women
who have learned to keep moving

and stay still at the very same time

WRITE A POEM SAID HAYDEN

about Hayden Carruth who had sat now
for hours drinking and talking
listening to the things I said

an hour I had thought maybe two
at the most but as the winds
began blowing the talk kept flowing

so Tom he said hands on the table
what should we have for dinner

Joe-Anne made fillet mignon
which I hadn't had in years
and as we finished he said
where's my birthday cake

Joe-Anne looked at me
slantwise and shook her head
it wasn't his birthday at all

but she happened to have cake
and served it with ice cream
and lit a single candle in each piece

we sang for the heck of it and ate

Joe-Anne said Hayden you are always
making up stories even though
he admitted later that they were true

well Hayden she answered you're always
making up facts which he also
acknowledged soon enough

we spoke of the origins of Pruiksma
and Carruth and how hard it is
to say with any certainty

nobody nobody really knows he said

we spoke of other poets living
and dead staying up till the winds
blew away my departure
and still his mind moved like a fox

a man is like a house
he said coming from the toilet
the first thing to go is the plumbing

later when Joe-Anne had gone up
to bed he looked at me
sphinx-like across the kitchen table
and said in a voice that I knew
from his poems I've been wrong
so many times and she's been right
so many times it makes her into
an ogre

      and he stopped
as I did hearing the word ogre
but only to catch his short breath

Pruiksma he said Pruiksma Pruiksma
that's a good name for an ogre

such was his poem about ogres
and friends sung as the winds
whipped round their house
and I sat without speaking
without lifting my glass
hoping the gale would never end

CHANGE OF PLANS

My father and his father
built a shed by our house
its roof at an angle complete
with an attic its own little door
a square with an X

they'd almost finished it
when the county came by
to say the new building
couldn't be where they built it
though no one in the office
had said it to my father
when he went there
two weeks before

but Grandpa was undaunted
and they set it on some pipes
rolling it with our neighbors
to the corner of the yard

where already someone else
had cut down the hedge
to make room for the shed
the great ship with barn doors
sailing the back yard the narrow
green sea then

coming to rest
in the newly cleared clearing
no longer at home at the edge
of our house but at least
still standing still a shed
in our yard

>   where it stands
> to this day though we moved
> somewhere else and no one there
> now knows the story

SUMMER SCHEDULE

The off-island biker
peers out at the water
upset the 10:50
hasn't come at 10:50

and no one to ask he
says to a tourist
and only one boat
he says to his phone

if he turned to his left
he'd see another ferry
pulling out on its way
from the dock to the island

late for the crowds that
come in late summer
but moving on the water
which keeps its own time

saying nothing to the man
still looking at his phone
for the boat that will never be there

MR. BERRY

A letter comes from Wendell
the old hero the old saint

who taught me far more
than I'd known I didn't know

and you would think I would celebrate
this gift of generosity

you'd think I wouldn't hesitate or be
nervous to open it

but I do and I am
and I wait the whole day

to follow the long lines
no less careful for their speed

where I read what I long
always to read

a voice speaking simply
of what matters beyond words

a man who means
each syllable he says

a person a poet
a farmer a friend

a gentleman of letters
who still writes his letters

disclosing his heart
with his hand

DAEMON

Gandhi did nothing
without hearing it speak
and sometimes heard nothing
and dared to do nothing
despite the many things
he may already have done

each day by listening
the battle was won
and not with any weapons
but by staying himself
saying his word
which said
no more than he heard

THE EYE THAT YOU SEE

for David

1

I have seen your eyes

they are green and brown

green at the edges
like algae like summer wheat

and brown at each center
a rust-colored corona
encircling a sun covered
by a moon

        except that
in their centers
I can find no moon

I look and I look
and I still want to look
at a darkness not dark
an emptiness not empty

a light I cannot see
that somehow sees me

I look into your eyes
and am seen

2

The eye that you see
sang Antonio Machado

poet of the man
who saw poetry
in me

the eye that you see
is not an eye
because you see it

standing
         reciting
the book worn to the page

it is an eye
an eye
saying it out loud
an eye

because it sees you

3

How long have I longed
to see an eye
            that sees me

to see myself
           within it
being seen
         being seen

I used to think it
only happened
in poems

4

I used to think
              so many things
only happened in poems

only poems
              contained clarity
clear enough to see

but you
        sweet poem
sweet song
            of my heart

you have seen it

you see it
        the world
as a poem

the world
        within me
as you see it
as you see

poetry
being born
all the time

5

I wish I could see it
all the time
            my sweet

I wish
I could gaze
   without end
into your eyes

    for they have
no end
  that my eyes
  can see

I wish
I could enter
the poem forever

forever
  seeing and
being seen

   6

Must I then
   imagine
the death of your eyes

the loss of their bright brown
green hazel fire

the loss of myself
peering out
from their centers

the loss
of a center
to see

7

The poem
          the poem

saying it
         out loud

the poem says yes

        you must

you must first
              imagine it

and then go on seeing

to see them
           each time
as miracle
        as light

a darkness not dark
an emptiness not empty

a poem
a song without end

SPRINGTIME IN THE CITY

is more than just city
though the city folks
see it as a sign to go out
to go shopping or sip wine
with others in the sun

and why wouldn't one
buy a few pleasures

but the boy on the hill
runs free of his mother
to dive with his fingers
into drifts of pink flowers
flinging with his fists
great flurries of petals
for a moment more free
than the air

A SENSE FOR THE MOUNTAIN

The mountain behind clouds
is no less a mountain
no less a giant peering forth
from above only now
we must see it with what
we have seen a presence
more present than sight

CARE

When I woke he was there
awake beside me
having slept on the floor
beside the long bed

I could feel the bandage
taped to my wound
only when I shifted
and turned in that bed

but I felt all over
my body still alive
with the life we shared
in sickness and in health

and the light I knew
there in his eyes
watching me
see him again

CASCADIAN LYRIC

After four days of rain
the light falls on green leaves
salal glowing brightly
almost from within
then fading with the sky
clouds moving in the leaves
not two things or one
but one moment unfolding
rain and sunlight and leaves
within it everything
within it without end

PRAYER

Our house was haunted
by perfection

not
    its attainment
but its ghost

how else could it pass
through walls without wavering
more fluid than heat or sound

nothing could be
what it was

always it
had to be better

spirit of attainment
attained without effort

perfect
imperfection

that quiets all ghosts

be
    with us here
as we make our new home

a home that can host
all beings at once

at one
in the dark
dark world

Thomas Hitoshi Pruiksma is an author, poet, translator, teacher, magician, musician, and lover of life. He was born in Seattle, Washington, and has lived and worked in Tamil Nadu, India, and Oaxaca, Mexico. His books include *Give, Eat, and Live: Poems of Avvaiyar* and *Body and Earth: Notes from a Conversation* (written with the artist C.F. John). He makes his home on Vashon Island, Washington, with his husband, David Mielke.

www.ingramcontent.com/pod-product-compliance
Lightning Source LLC
Chambersburg PA
CBHW021412290426
44108CB00010B/500